GO THERE

Aidan Rooney

MADHAT PRESS
CHESHIRE, MASSACHUSETTS

MadHat Press
PO Box 422, Cheshire MA 01225

Copyright © 2020 Aidan Rooney
All rights reserved

The Library of Congress has assigned
this edition a Control Number of
9781941196977

ISBN 978-1-941196-97-7 (paperback)

Drawings for *Fables* by Hammond Journeaux
Cover painting by Stivenson Magloire (1963–94), with
gratitude to Maria Isabel Moreno and Galerie Flamboyant,
9 rue Darguin, Pétion-Ville, Haïti
Cover design by Paul Kahn
Book design by MadHat Press

www.MadHat-Press.com

Introduction—Going for It

Go There, the title of Aidan Rooney's first collection to be published in the United States, voices an urgency that might be the poet mustering the inner resolve to embark on a journey of making, or it might be a call pitched outward to another, or others—the unknown place to which they are directed demands a crossing, and probably a transformation. Of course, the title requires us to read it both ways, and more, its richly reflexive play signaling the further journeys, historical passages, and border crossings of the poems that follow. Open yourself, free yourself, the epigraph from Jean Anouilh implies, the whole world is one step away. Go for it. Go there.

Aidan Rooney's first two books of poems, *Day Release* and *Tightrope,* published in Ireland, established him as one of the important Irish poets of his generation, a generation that includes David Wheatley, Conor O'Callaghan, Vona Groarke, and Justin Quinn, among others. What distinguishes him from his contemporaries, and still renders him something of an outlier, is his emigrant status outside the European Community. The poems of *Day Release* and *Tightrope* draw vitally from Rooney's experience growing up in Monaghan, notably a county of the Republic bordering Northern Ireland. Yet, these first books likewise include poems keenly influenced by his life as an emigrant in America, not entirely at home, though responsive to the immediacy and deep histories of place, society, and the personal stresses of life in a country of greater power and means than that of home. From this vantage, Rooney is at once Irish and Irish American, "both / and" rather than "neither one thing nor the other." *Go There* takes the inter-geographical and diasporic preoccupations of Rooney's first two books and extends them, extrapolates them into new geographical encounters and new imaginative possibilities.

The poems that open *Go There* place us in Rooney's first world of Monaghan, but even here the reader discovers foreshadowings of travels farther afield. The rabbits or connies, of the eponymous townland "Knockaconny" that the poet's ferret kills by the dozens become, deftly, harbingers of more distant sufferings intimated by Rooney's *Trócaire* box. Similarly, when a dead oak's nest of ants in "Colony" experiences its crisis, "the ones who can take wing to go elsewhere." The resonance with Irish history and colonization is understated here, but incontestable, as is the implied duplicity of who is colonizing whom, and the significance of the depiction quietly suggests wider contexts than the Irish alone. In addition, several poems early in the book recall the Troubles as encountered familiarly, while others look back into local history and ecclesiastical lore, themes that will surface again in poems like "The Eyes of St. Lucy" and "Patrick at Saint Honorat." By its end, *Go There* returns the reader to Rooney's first place in poems like "Happy Are They," as well as the beautiful and moving elegy for Seamus Heaney, "In a Country Churchyard," and the summarily panoramic "Sléibhín." The provocative slippages of this final poem offer an apt metaphor for the book as whole. Sléibhín means "little mountain," but it also is the name for a black-headed gull, and for a person who dissembles. The word itself, in short, is something of a shape-shifter, casting nets of meaning in multiple directions at once, crossing boundaries of definition.

It is this movement across boundaries, geographical, personal, communal, artistic, and linguistic that most characterizes the poems of *Go There*. Nowhere does the reader encounter this poet's intent to range imaginatively and formally, historically and politically than in the arc of poems that shapes the book's middle arrangement. European-based poems such as "Switzerland," "Skiing at Engelberg," and "Circuit," and North American poems such as "Seals," "In Acadie" and the exceptional "Habitation," poise the attentive reader for the series of moving poems prompted by Rooney's experience working in Haiti—among them "Angel," "Rigor," "You Just Might Find," "Billets Doux," and the title poem "Go There," a translation from the Kreyol of the Haitian poet Tontongi. It would be wrong to assume Rooney here is travelling genially across one border after another—the fictional voice that speaks from Nova Scotia's historical past exists in implicit dialogue with other colonizing voices as well as with the voices of the colonized, especially those of Haiti.

The poems "Patrick at Honorat" and "The Whispering Gallery at Grand Central" add the perspectives of fabled and contemporary journeys to this evocative mélange. The prayer whispered via a brilliant pair of couplets into the archway at Grand Central near the famous Oyster Bar in New York, a city of vast riches, echoes back to the whisperer because *no one was there.* Yet, the poet is there, and the poem pitched outward nonetheless stands as witness. The poems of Haiti, likewise, enrich themselves with the immediacy and vitality of lived experience. They are not tourist poems, but poems of intimate knowledge and connection. Nowhere is this more the case than in "Billets Doux" where the voice of the beloved speaks with tenderness and vulnerability through the medium, most unlikely, of an online exchange. This implied conversation appears at the center of *Go There,* as though at the heart of the book the poet wants to evoke the transformative power of human and artistic encounter.

It is not surprising, then, that translations also figure mightily in *Go There,* as do poems of ekphrasis. The sonnet sequence, "Nudes," for example, based on paintings by Edgar Degas, does more than simply represent the scenes depicted; Rooney, instead, weaves personal history through the scenes, as though to render the frames permeable to the poet's consciousness. Such poems are also crossings of a kind, as are the various translations, not least of which is "Go There" and "An Invitation to Leave," the first as noted from the Kreyol and the second from the French of Baudelaire. Exclusive of the English in which the poems of *Go There* are largely written, French, Irish, Kreyol, among others, find their place. Rooney's ability to range linguistically in the poems speaks to the kind of mutual "carrying across" embodied etymologically in the word "translation" itself. Finally, the formal variety of *Go There*, from sonnets, to the calligramme, "Malbec," to the experimental forms of "Longing" and "Quiz"—among a plethora of others—not only exemplifies Rooney's attention to craft but underscores, as well, his penchant for aligning a poem's shapeliness with his subject as expressively as possible. In doing so, the poems of *Go There* open the door to wider possibilities of regard for the reader, as much as for the poet. Or, as the final lines of "Patrick on Honorat" remind us:

> The splendor of the sun won't last.
> At my right and left stands fast
> God the one forever near
>   everyone
>   everywhere.

—Daniel Tobin

Table of Contents

Introduction—Going for It *by Daniel Tobin*	v
Knockaconny	1
Confession	3
Homework	5
Smigs	7
Colony	9
The Shoes	10
Recollection	12
Notice	13
The Intercessions of Saint Ciarán the Elder	14
Nudes	17
Switzerland	25
Skiing at Engelberg	26
The Eyes of Saint Lucy	28
Salut	30
Seals	31
Habitation	32
In Acadie	35
Go There	36
Patrick at Saint Honorat	37
Angel	39
Rigor	40
You Just Might Find	41
The Whispering Gallery at Grand Central	42
In Diquini	43
Billets Doux	44
Longing	54
An Invitation to Leave	55
Malbec	57
Synesthesia	58

A Day in Accordance with the Thirteen Virtues of Benjamin Franklin	59
Fables, *after Jean de la Fontaine:*	
1. The Fox and the American Chickens	61
2. The Old Cat and the Young Mouse	63
3. The Pig, the Goat and the Sheep	64
4. Two Mules	67
Revolution	68
The War Effort	69
4th of July	71
On Lovells	72
Happy are They	78
Nativity	79
Circuit	80
Lynx	81
Post-Op	82
The Mottoes	84
The Seventies	86
Quiz	87
Posts:	
1. On Religion	90
2. On Love	91
3. On War	92
4. On Death	93
Francis Bacon and the Hen	94
In a Country Churchyard	96
The Bones	97
Sléibhín	99
Acknowledgments	101
About the Author	103

*Franchir la porte, c'est tout un monde,
mais, en fait, il suffit de faire un pas.*

—Jean Anouilh, *La Valse des Toréadors*

Spaces left unfilled are as important as spaces filled.

—Sister Trea, Saint Louis Convent, Monaghan

Knockaconny

> *Cnoc na gCoiníní,* a townland
> north of Monaghan town

Whether we lived on a hill of rabbits
or of sticks was of some local debate.
I'd have favored *coinín* over *connadh,*
the ditches riddled, the fields overrun;
the dozens my ferret terrorized out
made no dent in the glut. At it, I thought,
they must have been, like rabbits, as I wrang
another neck and thrust it in the sack
so I wouldn't have to watch it quiver.

Once, I confessed to the murders, not long
before I gave the practice up. No harm
in that, assured the sympathizer priest
who had me do the creed for telling lies,
saying I'd forgotten my 2 new P
for the *Trócaire* box's black babies
when really I'd bought me an ice-lolly,
six smigs from The Heifer's bendiest strap
deemed, in the eyes of God, not near enough.

The bad ferret got taken to the vet,
and I took to whittling lengths of ash
to arrows whose butt-end I'd notch
to catch the gut that tautened in the bow
an alder branch became, the very ones
we sailed out over the Blackwater on

Aidan Rooney

and snapped off, the tree's tension re-released
on rabbits from as close as I could get.
But for all the sticks cut, not one caught.

Confession

Boys and girls, it started with, *take out your pencils,*
the thick carpenter ones we'd just used to copy
Ó Raibh Sé Do Bheatha Abhaile, then cut back
to the proper angle before putting them away.
Now, she said, *tear out a page from your copybook.*
First, we wrote by rote our art names in the top right.
I wrote *Degas.* Then, beneath that, *4A Ealaín,*
and *an 1 Feabhra, 1981,* beneath that again.
Now, she said. *Now,* with one of those full-stop pauses
she gave, looking out the window, to have us put
our thinking caps on. *Write,* she continued, *something
you want us to know about you we don't already.*
It was an odd question for back then, and took a bit
to figure out. Mushy McKenna started
knawing on his pencil and Pussy McGlone looked
like he always did, about to wet himself.
But, one by one, mostly the girls first, everyone
got stuck in. *Now,* pause, most of us already done,
*finish up and put your pencils down. Carefully,
fold up what you wrote as many times as you can.*
That too took a fair bit, folding our notes down
to little compressed accordions of paper.
Sister went on about Saint Brigid, us only half-
listening, having to weave her cross from rushes.
Now, she said, *stop folding.* Comiskey was not happy
because what he'd written you want people to know
they don't already know we all already knew,
the wanker, and was lying open on the table

Aidan Rooney

like a corrugated chessboard for all to see.
Now then. The real McCoy. Silence. Eternity.
*Tear another page out, and pick up your pencils,
please,* the *please,* unusual as it was, making us
a bit nervous. *Write something—no now, no pause—
about yourself you wouldn't want anyone to ever know.*
You could feel for a while everyone wondering
if Sister could be trusted, which we all did, before
we got down to writing it down, telling the truth,
the biggest confessions we'd ever made, the one
you thought of and immediately dismissed
waiting once a month to go *Bless me Father for
I have sinned,* knowing you'd get an eternity
of confiteors and sorrowful mysteries
of the rosary to the power of infinity.
I wrote something I still remember. *Now,* she said,
when all our pencils were put down all by ourselves
and we sat there like the final judgment,
tear what you just wrote into the smallest pieces.
After what seemed a short while, Corrigan went round
with the *bosca bruscair* and we cleaned up our mess.
Reid leant down and whispered *what the fuck's she up to*
through a cough. *Now, if you would all like to pass up
your folded notes, it would be lovely to know you
better.* We loved her even though you couldn't show it,
and she knew and knew why and how we couldn't.

Homework

Keep your head about you,
I hear my father say,
when I hang up the phone
and turn back to the end
of the evening news
and dinner with the boys.
I can't say I listened
much when he was alive,
the two of us well-versed
in the ways of the last child,
keeping cool and distant,
not needing many words.

The physician must think
me the right idiot
to think positive means
it will all be all right,
odd that I do not want
to come in right away.
The once I saw him cry
nearly moved me to tears.
He came home that night
from up at the County,
his son not an hour
detached from the machines.

Dishes in the washer,
ketchup in the fridge,

Aidan Rooney

everything put away
before we have ice cream,
then go over homework
the teacher will collect.
We sat at the table.
He wept into one hand.
All I could do was watch
and try to understand
the need to stay quiet,
to do it on your own.

Smigs

1. Once, for mitching Chem.

2. Each, me and Dolan,
the answer book stolen.

3. Scraping. Some B.S.
first day in C.B.S.
Who's the bees-knees?

4. Everyone in art,
dealt out when Treanor lit
a *Cara* up to light a fart.
Bull got a whiff of it.

5. Only. Swiss lost count.
I was about to mount
a ~~girl~~ bike (would you stop)
wasn't mine, on account
of a ride home, post-hop.

6. Of the best, all *ad hoc*.
A *cupla* lippy *foc-
ail* was all it took.
Real stingers. You felt your
heart in hands aswelter,
throbbing helter-skelter.

Aidan Rooney

7. Must have pulled a cute
one, cupped palm, given guff,
thought the six a right hoot.
Mea culpa, said frig,
got you one bonus smig.
Not even, understood,
must root bad out for good.

Colony

What I'd thought rot in the dead oak was ants,
the carpenter guild who'd bored the heartwood
the height of the trunk and out through the limbs.
They seethe from each break in the fallen tree,
like a smashed cantaloupe, down seed runnels,
in a stampede of black metallica.
Light-struck, the workers rise up on hind legs,
antennae hooked, and read the buzz-sawed air.

And here comes the queen, led forth in a convoy
of young swarmers laden with large, white eggs,
juggled between twins or backpacked aloft,
negotiating roadblocks and checkpoints,
the larvae cradled in the soft vice-grip
called for for infants and delicate weapons.
They will build upon a hill not far away.
The ones who can take wing to go elsewhere.

Aidan Rooney

The Shoes

Why did you have to tell me, Dad,
last night when I lined the shoes up
on the rack inside the front door,

about the time you gathered up
shoes blown out of their boxes
onto the street, and went about

the sorting on the footpath: first
into women, children, men; then
piles for gutties, casual, dress,

loafers, sandals, boots, hush-puppies,
wingtips, platforms, slippers, high-heels;
then ever smaller piles again

for same name-brand and colour;
then scrutiny for size on sole,
instep and under tongue; on then

into the putting into pairs
lined up the length of the street,
shop-front to curb, the footpath

chock-a-block with shoes you were let,
that afternoon, back in to sort
for the bomb-damaged markets,

GO THERE

the pick you had of Docs for pay,
and the cherry reds that took
a small forever, every time,

to lace up nice and snug
around the ankles, like the one
found attached that had no match.

Aidan Rooney

Recollection

> *Ramassez donc vos pêches*
> —"Les Pêches," André Theuriet

I met him just the once astride his horse,
looking for all the world the part of Lord.
A pack of hounds a fox had driven hoarse
wove beneath his boots a natural guard,
straying only to nose among the gorse.
I was headed home from his orchard
at the one point in a stream I could cross,
apples slung in the gut of my tee-shirt.

Decades later, one of those teaching lulls
when reading aloud brings on remembrance.
A fine day, young man, for picking apples.
I felt my blood rise, the ring of my silence.
His dogs went splashing past me where I stood
on a wobbly stone. Then the Lord rode homeward.

Notice

> Monaghan, *circa* 1720

The first Lord Bessmount had two lads lifted
in the matter of some cattle disappeared
that Indian summer. Assizes sieved
the evidence and found enough to rear
the thieves on high ropes in the Diamond.

Some who gathered were given to respond,
the town and times being tough, good riddance
to them both. Most cared less. The Lord knew well
to stay home in his Big House, keep his distance
along the slack Blackwater. A kind of hell
it turned, when out his woods, as winter neared,
several head of cattle reappeared.

Aidan Rooney

The Intercessions of Saint Ciarán the Elder

Ciarán of Saigir, *circa* AD 375-462

I.

One of the Carburys of Leinster once
took an unfortunate shine to a cow.
Whether he knew it belonged to the monks
is uncertain, but he slipped anyhow
into the byre under cover of darkness.
Noticing his finest milch-cow missing,
the morning milker made it his business
to notify Ciarán. Carbury was swishing
his way along with the cow up Slieve Bloom
when a cloud of mist and dark descended.
Torrential rain fell and formed a flume
that bore and turned the thief till nearly drowned.
And the cow found it in her capacity
to make her way back to the community.

II.

On another occasion, the Kearnes gang
crossed into Munster to raid some cattle.
A few locals joined a man called Longan
in pursuit, and no one rested up, not till
the Kearnes were up against a stand of trees
whose lower branches were slung with ropes.
The robbers begged Ciarán to intercede.
The monk recalled his early days, the high hopes
he'd had for the badger and the boar,
and the fox that stole and ate his sandals.
Impose your penance, the fox had implored,
and from then on, everyone became pals.
As do the two gangs when lightning flashes
between them. Everyone goes home and crashes.

III.

While still only a young boy on Cape Clear
where his parents had gone to bring him up,
away from it all among gorse and heather
before all that had become chic, the pup
the boy Ciarán was was out watching birds.
The hedgerows were profuse with the blood drops
of fuchsia, but the boy needed no words
or imagery when a black bird swooped
its talons down on a hatchling in its nest.
Who's to say what the boy felt, the chick borne
to a rock where the bird tore at its breast.
Or why the bird returned the corpse to Ciarán?
Arise, be whole, go, said the boy, opening the cage
of his hands around the chick that flew back to the hedge.

Nudes

after Edgar Degas

1. The Race / *Petites Filles Sportives provoquant des Garçons*

That that were us, down at the Convent Lake
a week before the Leaving, after art
with Sister Trea, where I'd have life-sketched
the deadly pout out of Angela's face
so she'd appear of this world, reachable,
more the *gamine des gamins de Montmartre*
we all were, even the Muck McKenna,
than the epitome she was to me
of cool and class and real unhappiness,
when we took the notion to do something
wild and wonderful, daredevil to strip-
tease out of the uniforms we hated,
and take to the haunted waters in a race
around the crannóg and back before the bus.

2. The Dance / *Petites Paysannes se baignant à la mer vers le soir*

The decades, give or take, to set things right,
repopulate a strand that flopped with fish
the sucked-back sea cast up before the quake
with girls naked for no one but themselves
in surf that's up this evening even if
the sun gives the impression it's gone down
in the diesel-spewing port of Jacmel,
and will do all it can to cool the fire-
storms of revolutions raged so long
what else can three girls do but want someone
to paint them crudely in in a hurry,
lashings of roasted cocoa, coffee, sugar,
rinsed of coal and salt and scorched-earth lime,
at close of day, dancing into the dark.

3. The War / *Scène de guerre au moyen age*

Given the hard-to-figure-out décor,
you could be forgiven for mistaking
this this-is-our-land war for something else,
an *In Arcadia Est* set upset
by a fox-hunting party headed home,
not one not worth a single drop of blood
apparent, one androgynous hunter,
granted, about to let an arrow go
into a girl who looks like she's just stepped
from a bath and wants a towel handed,
a kind of calm-cum-calamitous cast
to the victims lying in such poses
girls can strike, getting ready to go out
or go to sleep, or play, as one does, dead.

4. Interior / *L'Intérieur*

This is a novel I have put away,
too naturalist by far and *clair-obscur*,
best lost in an unconfessional file
where the real and the theatrical blur,
so that even you have to ask yourself
who misbehaved, because some one, at least,
has, by the looks of things, the not a lot
of love in the room with a narrow bed
where, were it not for the one cold shoulder,
the characters keep a lot of clothes on,
the plot so wrought with conflicting sources
it would be wrong to come down too hard
on she who'll want to pull herself together
or he who has his back against the door.

5. The Bath / *Femme dans son bain*

As much as a man likes a woman
statuesque and ripped, the warrior-slash-
goddess sort who's possibly bionic,
in nothing but a loincloth and a spear,
there's a lot to be said for an idle
lover, every other weekend, who lies
about the house between the meals and sex,
wholesome, elaborate, à la carte,
her skin as soft and as easily bruised
as a nectarine or over-ripened pear,
her limbs in the constant off-kilter state
of a sufferer from some vague tristesse,
akimbo or curled under, or stretching
the way a dancer in a bathtub must.

6. The Lesson / *L'Etoile*

When Mélanie, once, in the entr'acte
of *le show* at the *Paradis Latin*,
showed me how to cancan *en pointe* then split
before the gypsy caravan scene,
it cost me the double shift in wages docked
when we lined up before the brute *Le Buffle*
who put me in mind of the Bull McCague
sending me down the over a hundred
Christian Brothers steps to buy a spirit
level bubble from Hughie the Bucks,
up to his old codology of tricks,
the Bull himself counting out *as gaeilge*
six smigs for mitching Irish, that still sting
every time I watch ballet or opera.

7. The Split / *Après le bain, femme nue s'essuyant la nuque*

When the first marriage went south and we got
to divvying the spoils of fourteen years—
armoires, beds and bureaux, the chinaware
and cutlery, drapery, etc.,
an alphabet of stuff accrued and shared
all the way to the zip saw in the shed,
then the weeks the parenting plan agreed
each of us would spend with or without the boys,
and on into the personal effects,
to each one's own, clothing, books, CDs, skis,
till we got to the artwork on the walls,
—you went for the Toulouse-Lautrec *Toilette,*
and I Degas's, both here, side by side,
in a rare, occasional exhibit.

8. Interior II / *Rolla,* Henri Gervex

No matter Degas's advice to Gervex
to paint an undone corset on the floor
into the indications of consent,
the beaux-arts crowd deemed the scene indecent,
the girl on the white bed too resplendent
with all her gems and posh apparel off,
the very picture of satisfaction
most men and women want to get and give,
and the romanced end, no less, of a poem,
the man at the window beside himself,
broke from a bout of wantonness, and about
to do away with himself with poison,
all why, for months in the dealer's window,
the painting enjoyed a non-stop procession.

Switzerland

Helvetia auf der Reise,
—Bettina Eichin (sculptor), Basel

She sits above the river in the stance
of one who does not care to be approached.
The cloak she's taken off, the shield and lance
that, were she to be bothered, lie in reach,
have taken on that sickly, lichen hue
soldiers her age used burnish to erase.

As has her suitcase squarely placed nearby,
the standard issue sort between the wars
people could comfortably carry far.
Her feet are bare, as if she might descend
to dip them in the slow river's solder,
lose track awhile of how such journeys end.

Aidan Rooney

Skiing at Engelberg

> *And men go about to wonder*
> *at the heights of the mountains*
> —Saint Augustine, *Confessions*

When you look around in the gondola,
not to mention *out,* on the last cable
to the peak, taking, as ever, the *voilà*
top-of-the-world outlook of the able,
you start to think you're more than a little
in over your head. Picks and shovels, an awl,
a knife I saw a man with once whittle
down a tuna. But no. *It is a snow-saw,*
the German, French, or Swiss responded,
in a singsong tone that put the blade right
at home in a playground. We bonded
as the gondola rose into the high light
summits are, and I became less conscious
of my tame, rented gear that had *Titlis,*
the name of the mountain, written on it.
I could tell I was part of an unwitless
and undead serious skier chapter
less by the Volkls, Rossis and Salomons,
and the red and red-crossed helicopter
dropped to a pad a ski patrol slalomed
elegantly to with a casualty
in tow, than by how, communally, all tuned
to updates on conditions, the quality
of terrain and snow. You'd swear it was the moon
we were climbing to for all the talk

Go There

of crags and craters. The car had turned
360, rocked, and faced into sheer rock
when my snow-saw friend saw fit to turn
the talk to the slopes most recent mishaps:
the expert who'd simply disappeared last spring;
an avalanche that overtook two chaps
dug out when someone made a cell-phone ring;
and the gentleman not a month ago
who vanished into a transverse crevasse.
Everyone nodded in assent as fresh snow
began to plummet decidedly past
where we scaled ever higher to the top.
A witness noted where he'd disappeared,
and when the rescue squad arrived they dropped
ropes as far as they would fall. One appeared
to answer with the weight of a happy man
eased to safety. A snow bridge had caved,
he reported, but he'd been lucky to land
on an ice-flange not too far down. It saved
him from the plight of the not-so-fortunate skier
he too had just watched plunge past into the glacier.

Aidan Rooney

The Eyes of Saint Lucy

> *Saint Lucy* (circa 283–304), martyr, and patron saint of the blind.
> *Saint Lucy's Eye* is the mother-of-pearl cover of a winkle found along the French Riviera and carried as an amulet.

> *nobis quoque peccatóribus*

As if about to make in her diary
a brief entry of little consequence,
she raises in one hand a quill of palm.
In the other she offers, like glasses
idly doffed the better to recollect,
a posey of her own two hazel eyes
hanging in petals from a single stem.

She writes the names we answer absent to
in Fieri and Zagreb, weight and height,
codes for comeliness of mouth and eye,
and to take the edge off a cutting look
she adds a soft *sfumato* touch. *J'accuse*,
they seem to say offhand, their gaze gone hard
en route via Syracuse to Marseilles.

Two for ten at market in the *Vieux Port*
where fishermen pour *rascasses, rougets, vives*
out of buckets onto trays the monger sieves
to splay, one-eye-up, in the long *presque mort*
fish go through out of water. Select one

for fortune, girls, and a second to tuck
on a night out, in a friend's backpocket.

A powerboat's buzz does little to report
the displaced ones she keeps her eyes out for,
their *via crucis* lightened between visits
by silver set to sizzle in a spoon.
It dulls the eyes held *entr'ouvert* for days,
restores enough the girl knocked out of them
to interest that off-white, off-shore yacht.

Crowned in thorns, urchins on the halfshell
top a basket of uncleft *fruits de mer,*
their briny sweet shucked nothings laid bare
on mother-of-pearl. *Dé-li-cieux,* he says,
a bunch of fingertips blossoming forth
from a kiss his lips mimic … *mais, monsieur,
il faut que vous en mangiez plusieurs.*

Extracted thus, these eyes can look so right
through you you have to look the other way,
pray, if you get your tongue back, they'll grow back
full and clear-cut in the head, ready to choose
which *porte-bonheur* to hold sun and seaward,
to enter how they are and swerve to motion, color, light,
and have the nerve to turn in everyone in sight.

Aidan Rooney

Salut

after Stéphane Mallarmé

Nothing, this foam, but verse, first draft,
that works itself out in the flute
the way some seals, far off, afloat,
form a mostly belly-up raft.

We set sail, O my diverse, daft
friends, I already on the boot,
you on the swank prow of the boat
that cuts through winter's lightning draught;

a sweet drunkenness urges me
despite the surges of the sea,
to raise this toast, this *salut*—

solitude, reef, starburst—
to whatever measures up to
the blank canvas of our artwork.

Seals

At first there is just you,
your black eyes fixed on me,
breaching in the same spot
we said goodbye last fall
as if like me you'd like
to ask: is that you again?

Then, alongside the Glades,
a clatter of spring pups
vie to climb up onto
a tilt of ledge low tide
has exposed, reign a while
then slither back to water.

I paddle past but note
how you have multiplied
to two, four, eight poked heads,
treading water round me
at every compass point
with not so much as a splash.

I turn and scull beyond
the Grampus rocks to beach
in a secluded cove.
Driftwood. Bait bags. Golf balls.
Storm-battered lobster traps.
Great tangles of frayed rope.

Aidan Rooney

Habitation

Le Nouveau Monde, 1605–13

I.

Forsaking that cold and scurvy island,
we crossed the *Baie Fendu* to *Port Royal,*
and cleared of virgin spruce a rise designed
for habitation. The smith poured oil
on whipsaw blades our dogs got set to shove.
The savage came and watched the carpenters
peg mortise to tenon, raise beams above
the trading room we built to splay their furs.
We had our negro speak for us to them
in smidgens of Basque and Mi'qmaq tongue.
In time, we would get along. Their *sachem*
liked the looking glass, the knife of iron,
the copper kettle in which he wet a tea
from needles of the arbor vitae tree.

II.

One man, each evening, wore around his neck
the collar of the Order of Good Cheer.
The savage called him *Atoctegic,*
he who rules the banquet. The day before,
he'd hunt down prize meats, then stick sticks through
orifices of gutted coons and geese,
the great cage of a moose or caribou,
and take these to the cook's rotisseries.
It came our negro's turn to rule the feast.
He'd learned the savage tongue, and how to spice
beaver meat with chervil, clove and pepper.
Some stood round. The women wove, and men passed
pipes, watching the manner of our service.
We gave them bread as one would do the poor.

III.

The fog that morning held outside the gut.
The basin swelled. A savage blew his horn.
We did the scraps of last night's banquet up
to take with scythes upriver to the corn.
We cropped till turn of tide, loaded, returned
to Habitation. The scent of smoke
smote us first, birch and spruce, the place burned
to its saw-pits. The savage showed and spoke
pidgin to our negro. The furs and fish,
all taken, right down to our moccasins.
White, we learned in French, but different tongue.
And wild, the negro said. Sounds like English.
We had to let the savage take us in.
They sat round fires. They shucked the corn to song.

In Acadie

There is an interior here new world
blow-ins like myself don't enter often,
a dark sky reserve one can paddle round
like a first person. I like how round here
they will say, *I'm going up the valley,*
the way we would go—our home on a road
that took a fair dip out front—*down the North.*
We'd make a list. I'd to hide the butter.

The Home Depot an hour up the valley
has everything every Home Depot has
to put up a house, and then some, *mod-cons*
you'd call them. Onward, an airport. You'd land
in for the best, one-month summer around,
this only the half of it. You should see
the holiday home, not the one you saw,
once, really, only. You came across as

lonely for your own home. There's a county
near here, funny—Clare County—like back home
but backward. We never knew if it was you
after it or both of you for the saint.
I've a friend in Clare; she speaks a mix of
Mi'qmaq and French, English like ours. You'd love
the wild life: porpoises, given the tides,
owls, wolves, the odd howl from who or God knows what.

Aidan Rooney

Go There

after the Haitian Kreyol of Tontongi

Go there, where you know yourself
you should, before the sad sack
of your heart withers tighter
than the skin on a bodhrán.
Go there, even if you're ticked off
at policy, even if you turn to salt
at the who's-who fundraiser feast.
You have to go there, brothers, sisters,
where nobody gives the destitute
the time of day,
where no light lights
their day with hope.
Go there, bring your zeal to bear
on the happiness of other people.
Fight and right the wrongs
the world's poor endure
as if they'd no business being here at all,
here where, with plenty, the splendour falls.
You have to go there, stay there, join us
if only with a soft smile on your mouth.
O my sisters, my brothers, we are needed there
to plant together, without any more shenanigans,
oranges and corn and friendship
for all of us on earth who need relief.

Patrick at Saint Honorat

I am of nowhere everywhere here,
crude in things, God the sphere
of water round me, sky above,
      a career
        I have tired of.

I am the no one no one goes near.
Other brothers steer clear
of my dark cell, night walks,
      God in my ear
        tall talks.

I am of nowhere everywhere here,
full and bereft of fear,
God before me against ill,
      all-seer,
        always still.

I am the no one no one goes near,
rude becomes me and desire
to know God in me invisible:
      love and I are
        indivisible.

I am of nowhere everywhere here,
drawn in dreams home where
heathens in the woods meet
      God on earth
        beneath their feet.

The splendor of the sun won't last.
At my right and left stands fast
God the one forever near
      everyone
        everywhere.

Angel

Her ankle tag reads *Ange-Louise, 2 ans.*

Were it not for the diaper in her frock
she'd slip. She sleeps in the crook of my arm,
also fallen asleep. Her sweat beads grow.

She'd be one of the ones on the world news
had she not hung her eyes and raised her arms
for nothing more than a pick-me-up.

Were it not for her heat and her heartbeat
against mine, she might not be there at all.
There are no words. Outside, a waiting truck.

I hope she won't wake when I put her back.

—*L'Orphelinat Mère Térésa, Port-au-Prince, 2012*

Aidan Rooney

Rigor

All I can say to her in her language
is: this will pass. The tremors run through her
as if the earth had started up a dance,
then she dozes again under my hands,
good for nothing but their light-press weight.
Her too-small infant coos in the next room.
Sa a ap pase, I want to soothsay
in a more inarticulate Kreyòl
when the rigor roils again and her eyes
reopen into mine. Glazed. How can fear
appear so beautiful? There is nothing
more to say, so I say: *Dòmi, Couche.*
Couche, Dòmi, I say again, when we drop
her and her baby home—an 8-foot cube,
corrugated tin, US AID
wrap round bamboo stakes—and go over
the medications she will need to take,
counting out the days—*demen, aprè demen*—
till she is well and I will be long gone.

You Just Might Find

You can't always get what the world needs now
when you're living in your own private now
or never. A team of wild horses couldn't get no
satisfaction. Hey hey, bye bye, ain't no
sunshine of my life. All I want to be
's an American I'm afraid of, be
a complete unknown, hold your hand, get real,
real gone. Something in the air. How does it feel?

Imagine all the people. How many times
can a man sleep tonight, let the good times
roll around the clock? Every breath you take
disregards the rest. Walk this way or take
the long way home. Try some time. We've only
just begun to own a broken heart. So lonely.

Aidan Rooney

The Whispering Gallery at Grand Central

Into one corner outside the Oyster Bar
I closed my eyes and whispered just one prayer.

It shot across the archway like a star
then back to me because no one was there.

In Diquini

In a passionate, long-cambering bid
to make it out onto the Saint Rock road
and up the mountain, past boys on hunkers
outside Baptist and Adventist churches,
breaking rubble down to rock and aggregate,
past the Miami numbers chalked on slate,
past grazing pigs and cocks, past the beatings
oil drums get in Fair Trade Art, the bleatings
of Pay-1-Forward goats, across from *Père
Eternel* Auto Body Parts Works, over
the hospital wall, top-dressed in cement
and the halves of broken bottles, hell-bent
on getting out, unscathed by razor-wire
snagged on rusted, twisted pegs of rebar,
and looking to graft itself from you to me,
the bougainvillea, in Diquini.

Aidan Rooney

Billets Doux

for Darline

1.

How I would love so much
to breathe your mountain air.
You say you miss me but I miss you more.
It wasn't the same at the hospital today
now that you have gone back far.

I will never be far.
You have only to ring me and I will be there.
I hope to see you again soon. I want your snow.
Carry yourself well and take care.
Sleep well above all.

Thank you for thinking of me above all.
When I was with you it was my first work.
Not long ago I thought even God doesn't see me.
I hope to work soon since I feel free working.
I wish you an agreeable day, my dear.

Your advice to me is dear.
You are not leaving me tonight:
you are just going away a while.
Hug for me those close to you
although they do not know me.

It seems to me that you know me.
Your *coucou* this morning made me laugh.
I do not want to bother you often
for fear you'd feel the need to answer.
I will be wise like an image.

2.

My battery is up, my friend,
and the electricity is down again,
but leave me still your message.
I will have the pleasure of reading it
under the diamond light of the stars.

I like to feel the vigor of the stars.
The night sky is a corner I escape to.
I open my mouth to see the future.
You did not see it but I was desperate.
One more time, *bisous*.

A moonlight kiss. I kiss you
one hundred times plus one.
I would love to see the world.
Maybe you can bring just my eyes with you.
I thought about you the whole day.

Good day, my friend. Know that not a day
goes by that I do not think of you.
I beg you never leave my heart alone.
I spend my day checking my messages
hoping for just one *coucou* from you.

Go There

I kiss you and hope it draws a smile from you.
A smile from you would melt my heart.
I am happy I am missed by you.
Sleep well, my dear. A big hug.
My land misses you like water.

3.

It is morning for me also.
I have closed the doors to the house
and have only books and pen for friends.
I am tired of the glimmer of despair
outside in the eyes of the young.

I love books but here the young
choose careers based not on interest
but stability. I find in you that friend
who can light the rude path. Goodnight.
Bisous. Your words are the best gifts.

I have never received a gift.
Or post. That I count makes me smile
like never. To send a book would be hard.
Addresses here are complicated
because of how the houses are disposed.

Tonight I deposit
a kiss of friendship on your cheek.
Please do not let go my hand.
Tell me that I will see you soon.
I hug you hard, tender friend.

Go There

I have to go get water, dear friend.
Anyway, I have no more battery.
I will copy the Baudelaire onto a page
to have it more often under my eyes
and not go through your messages.

4.

Sometimes I break my head
to comprehend your words.
I would pay blood to leave this labyrinth.
To stay, as you say, as I am
is to stay weak, to stay with fear.

Tonight you calm my fear.
Your words are like a fine rain
that falls on every flower of my day.
It is as if you understand me
as much as or more than I do.

No one needs you more than I do.
Today it is so hot we suffocate.
I would love so much to find myself
in the cold with you beneath covers,
your body close to mine. Are you leaving?

Ouf, relieved. I did not want you to leave
and my imprudence be the fault.
I love you much, you know.
Your whenever you want will take some time.
I will come to you in your dreams.

Coucou! Last night, you visited my dreams.
I have gone over the unedited pages
of our *billets doux*.
You are more intimate to me
than you could ever imagine.

5.

Your words for you and I,
our I-don't-know, tear at my spirit.
Why do you have to kill the joy
by talking about the differences?
Goodnight, my dear. Sleep well.

I have a fever and did not sleep well.
You will not have to send your cold cloth caresses.
When you get home I will be waiting for you
on the bed with an embroidered sheet.
You will take my hot and hold me close to you.

Me too, I want you close to me.
I have limited myself till now
to watching you behind glass.
I have the desire to touch you tonight
but the fear of breaking everything.

To me you are everything.
I am letting go your hand
to caress and kiss your neck.
It is to dare, my dear, my secret,
my buried dream, my promised land.

Go There

No more distance, no more rules. Promise.
I take you in my heart and in my body.
We will go where languages end
and visit the country of stars.
You will take me by the hand.

Longing

She'll	*lu-*	*de*
e-	*on-*	*nous*
mail	*go,*	*deux*
me,	*en*	*nus,*
I	*tout*	*des-*
guess,	*cas,*	*sous*
my	*to*	*des-*
es-	*a-*	*sus,*
press-	*rouse*	*bun-*
o	*id-*	*os-*
so-	*ées*	*cionn,*
so,	*à*	*ver*
mais	*mi-*	*sur*
trop	*di*	*ver.*

An Invitation to Leave

after Charles Baudelaire

    My young one, my love,
    think, were we to leave,
how sweet it would be, how true,
    to love at leisure,
    to love and die there
in a country just like you.

    Sunrays through a shower
    the sky cast over
have, for me, all the allures
    your eyes possess
    each time they flash
enigmatically through tears.

There, nothing but composure,
    lush beauty, peace and pleasure.

    Furniture that wears
    the polish of years
would decorate our chamber;
    flowers from afar
    would add their odor
to fragrances of amber.

    Ceilings extraordinaires,
    the deepest mirrors,
the oriental opulence,

Aidan Rooney

    all articulate
    the soul's secret
in its own native cadence.

There, nothing but composure,
    lush beauty, peace and pleasure.

    See those canals lift
    the drowsy boats that drift
wherever the mood inspires;
    they gather here
    from all over
to soothe all your desires.

    The sun going down
    dresses each town,
canal and outskirt meadow
    in hyacinth and gold;
    the whole world
sleeps in a warm glow.

There, nothing but composure,
    lush beauty, peace and pleasure.

Malbec

    In color,   intensely
     indigo   close to glass.
  Nose, notes of   blueberry,
 black cherry,   violets,
white pepper.   In the mouth,
fresh, lush,   boysenberry,
raspberry,   blackberry,
 giving way   to hints of
  chocolate   and mocha.
   Enjoy with: chorizo;
    ripe cheeses;   rare red meats;
      pan-seared *foie de veau,*
        sauce madère;
       Or enjoy
       on its
       own,
       on
       your
       own,
     its whole
      world
       in
      your
      hand
    like one big
   bloodlet drop
  about to   rerelease
in one long, jammy, connected finish.

Aidan Rooney

Synesthesia

A ripe *Banon* or a *Vache de Charlais,*
right out of its chestnut leaves, can parley

the uddery bouquet of cows and goats
into taste. About as good as it gets.

A Day in Accordance with the Thirteen Virtues of Benjamin Franklin

Oatmeal, yogurt, blackberries and coffee
to start, peace and quiet, *The Boston Globe*.
Pick up a bit before some frontal lobe
resolve kicks in, to-do lists, stickies, who
to have for lunch on day-old ratatouille
or a chowder built from last Sunday's dig.
Connect. Like a lot. Heel your attack dog
but shame on us our last catastrophe.
Afternoon recovery nap. A swim
and steam at the local Y. Long hot shower.
Evening's door left open to a whim
of venery, no more than a happy hour.
Down, then, to work, humanity's riot
with the vanities, laying no store by it.

Fables

after Jean de la Fontaine

1. The Fox and the American Chickens

A fox signaled apocalypse
to turkeys who sought roost and refuge in a tree.
The rogue roved the ramparts around their acropolis
    and, seeing each bird stand sentry,
cried out: *who are these folk who dare make me look dense!*
Give me one reason to show them jurisprudence!
No way! Heaven forbid! He would get the job done
in spite of a full moon that up till then had shone
its favor on the turkeys more than on *Your Liege.*
    Being no novice to the art of laying siege,
the fox dug deep into his bag of blackguard tricks.
First he feigned climbing, then strapped his legs to sticks;
for a while he simulated death, then bounced right back.
    Houdini himself couldn't hack
    half the outfits he went through.
He backed up his *derrière,* set his tail ablaze,
    one of hundreds of circus *coups.*
Meanwhile, not one bird plucked the courage up to snooze:
the enemy fox wore them down keeping their focus
on his constant hocus-pocus.
The poor pluckers, in due course, fell into a stupor,
and dropped down one by one. The fox proved a trooper.
    He fell to each one till near half the troupe lay slain,
whereupon he dragged them to his winter storage bins.
Too much attention paid to all the danger signs
and we get what we have coming.

2. The Old Cat and the Young Mouse

A young mouse with not a lot of experience
thought it could coax a cat to show some forbearance
by reasoning with old Mr. Mistoffelees:
> *Please let me live; a mouse my size*
> *who eats next to nothing amounts*
> *to how much in this enterprise?*
> *What drain am I on the big cheese,*
> *his lady or their entourage?*
> *A grain of wheat more than does;*
> *a nut and I become huge.*

Right now I'm no better than a lite hors-d'oeuvre;
think to when you'll sire, sir, and keep me in reserve.
Thus, being in a bind, the mouse spoke to the cat
> who was having none of it.

You might as well address, Mouse, the hearing-impaired
as submit to me, Cat, your discourse of the scared.
I'm of the sort, not to mention age, for whom grace
> *is absurd. Therefore, down you go.*
> *Die. Save your breath for the trio*
> *'Destiny's Child'; they'll salve your case.*

As for my offspring, I'm sure other mice will show.
> There you have it. As for an ethic,
insofar as only one is evident:
youth loves listening to itself being confident;
> age is unsympathetic.

3. The Pig, the Goat and the Sheep

Together with a fat pig, a sheep and a goat
traveled in a trailer on its way to market,
in order to be sold, no pretense made about
any entertainment. They could forget all that;
the drover harboured no intent
of showing them the circus tent.
    Prince Porky squealed when off they went
as if, in some past life, a butcher'd hacked his trotters.
He put up such a racket it drove people deaf.
The other animals (kinder, gentler creatures),
good folk, wondered why he cried for help;
they could see no reason to be afraid.
    The drover said to the pig: *You're driving us all mad*
    with your incessant complaining? Give it a rest.
Take a page from these two. They could keep you honest,
teach you a thing or two, at least to hold your tongue.
Take, for example, the sheep; has he said one word?
He is wise.
           —*He's a turd,*
returned the pig. *If he's honest, he'd take the bung*
out of his thrapple and act like he's frightened.
As for your other royal highness,
Puck, he'd do well to do likewise.
They think they're headed to be enlightened,
the sheep of his fleece coat, the goat of his milk load.
That, I don't know. But being good
for little but being edible,
my death is inevitable.

Au revoir *roof above my head!*
 Thus reasoned Prince Piggy, this being his nature.
But what good did it do him? Whining makes no sense,
and bad luck will not be stayed by fearful prescience;
those who look ahead the least are the most mature.

4. Two Mules

Two mules were on their way, one laden with oatmeal,
    the other with sacks of cash labeled: IRS.
Not for all the world would this glorious half-ass
let his load be lightened. This was such a big deal.
    Out front he rang his little bell
    in lock-step strut revival,
    when suddenly someone put paid
    to his I-have-it-all parade.
A band of bandits pounced, grabbed him by his bridle;
    fiscal government went idle.
    The mule put up a fight and brayed
past every stone they threw at him, whinging, moaning:
So this is what, says he, *I had coming to me?*
That mule knows too well to fall back from my stoning,
    stay the course, get to be let free.
    —*Listen, pal,* his friend responded,
It's not always great to have a boss in high places:
If you had served, like me, the hard-working classes,
    you might not be so despondent.

Aidan Rooney

Revolution

    after Francisco Goya

Little unimaginable happens
anymore. One moment you're splitting tapas
in a downtown bar in Basra or Barça,
some rococo joint near a fallen palace,

the next, the lad who holds your horses has
summoned some local half-assed militia
to bring it on, the scarlet brouhahas
of reprisal, street by street, the lanterns high.

And there always will be we who don't so take
that kindly to enlightenment we'll baulk
at rounding up last night's insurgents to take
them away from the darkened town to talk.

One in an excruciatingly white chemise
does no one in attendance a disservice
throwing his arms up at the guns, going, *fire, please,
as soon as you see the colour of my eyes.*

The War Effort

I.

In the end it fell to Cincinnatus.
He was staking a ditch around his farm
of four unsown acres when the senators
approached to ask he intercede. Great harm
has fallen the Republic, they pleaded,
the army's been besieged. Cincinnatus
wiped himself of dust and sweat, and needed
only to fetch his toga from the house
before he crossed the river. In the city,
he suspended all civil business
and attendance to private activity.
Thus, all able joined with Cincinnatus
in the expedition. It took just one shout
to turn the enemy camp's attention inside out.

II.

The enemy entreated Cincinnatus
to show forbearance, not to slaughter all.
He made the generals pronounce they'd lost
the war, and had them marched to Rome in thrall.
All enemy combatants were made strip,
face the way they'd come. Cincinnatus staked
two spears in the muck, one across the top.
No sooner had they passed beneath his yoke
when the Senate received his *fasces,* an axe
bound in a bundle of rods. Word was out
he'd split the spoil among his men, then made tracks
for home. That the farmer was not an hour
in the door when he went out to his byre to yoke
twin oxen to the traces of his plough.

4th of July

> *Do you mean, citizens, to mock me?*
> —Frederick Douglass, July 5, 1852

A redneck in a shock of silver hair
at the wheel of a dark blue Escalade
with front and back vanity license plates
for veteran / ex-prisoner of war,
notices one not long back from the war,
headed to fireworks on the esplanade,
a bit banged up, a do-rag where the plates
do well to keep him pumping in his chair.
The elder parks, then parks his folding chair
alongside his inheritor, and waits
for the long overture to escalate
its fussy pastoral to scores of war,
to lean in and shout above the riproars
of cannon on the river: *this day is yours.*

Aidan Rooney

On Lovells

1.

Saltspray rose has breached the island's batteries.
It drops antennae down the hot concrete
of pits that housed the disappearing guns,
explodes in butterflies of pink and white
beneath winged sumacs anchored in the cracks.
A long sun-spell has scorched all grass and moss,
all bar the marrams that bunker down the dunes,
to shades of russet crisp around the tent.
It bristles underfoot then thins to sand
that could not give more dessicately hot
between your toes. All paths lead to beach save
the lane of broken asphalt that takes a dip
through saltmarshes, then rises to span
the island's drumlins wrapped in parapet.

2.

The harbor swells, strewn at every bearing
with islands a glacier ebbing inland
let go of. Bedrock and till. In the west,
the city stacks it oblongs in a maze
the Charles and the Mystic glister through
to swill their watersheds in the ocean.
Across the Narrows, ramparts top the cliff
of George's, its cannons long airlifted.
Gull-wail above the Brewsters to the east,
where the New World's first beacon upholds
its appearance of keeping watch. All about,
the islands appear to disengage and lift.
The tide engulfs tombolos, swallows spits,
resaturates and sets driftwood to drift.

3.

A wind-shift whips the flysheet to a sail
that tugs as if to pitch the tent elsewhere.
The captain's letters reveal that such a turn,
and lack-reaction from a sleeping crew,
had caused the *Magnifique* to run aground
on a shoal off the island's northwest end.
Without so much as a shiver or a heave
she came to rest. By high tide she'd filled,
all hands abandoned ship, and salvagers
culled her cannon for the *America*.
The island rose as if it felt the nudge
of ice again, then fell back into form.
You've come to feel the lurch beneath the bar
that silted over the lost man-of-war.

4.

A *Visitors Exercise Caution* sign
on Gallops lies face-up in poison ivy.
All rooves along Main Street have fallen in.
In front of the Union soldiers' mess hall
re-leased to the post-war Radio School
lilac and mock orange hold out against
encroachments of chokecherry. Privet
has pushed the path up around the doctor's house
whose bricks bulge out of bond and teeter
along the tops of walls about to cope.
A passing lobster boat impersonates
suppressed coughs from the quarantine station
as if the warden could any moment call.
Out back, snowberry soothes the cemetery.

5.

Without having to be told, the children
perform their disappearing act. They've gone,
as kids to waters' edges always have,
to skip their hard-sought-after rocks, call out
a record number. Thompson's Asylum
for Boys' boys needed constant breaking up
and packing off, sullen-faced, to be beaten
at the former Prisoner of War Barracks.
The water licks the slates of Bumpkin's beach
where boys and girls were set to wait their turn
to be carried aboard the yacht *Aztec*.
They watch as nurses help the soldiers up
the slope to the Home for Crippled Children.
And wonder when, if ever, they'll be back.

6.

On Lovells, too, the water-taxi drops
new overnighters off. A ranger asks
that all one's stuff brought on gets taken off.
You've left no mark. You put in and point home,
light and level in your kayak, well clear
of least terns the island's heirloom rabbits
are bent on decimating. Past Lovers Rock
from which a couple waves and you wave back.
Past The Point where bales of pitch and ocre
burned in an iron well. And past, last before home,
Sarah overrun with birds. White egrets stand
in the dead elm, cormorants in the oak.
One on a rock splays itself above the sunset gloss
making for you the crude rune of one black cross.

Aidan Rooney

Happy are They

after Joachim du Bellay

Happy are they—like Ulysses or your man
who won the fleece, lads after an expedition—
who can go home full of grace and dedication,
and spend their golden years surrounded by their own.
 When, I wonder, will I look down on my home town,
the smoke from out its chimneys, and in what season
see again the door of the house I grew up in?
A bungalow, but the world to me and then some.

Would the home my family made make me more glad
than this big house with its manicured façade?
Can marble hold a candle up to hand-cut slate?
Would the Blackwater sing more than the North River?
Or the black hills there win over the Blue Hills here?
Either way. I'd not corrupt the sweet air there with salt.

Nativity

The crib figures are just as you'd suppose
in Tintoretto's late *Nativity*.
They gather round the lime-lit baby,
the picture of the just-been juxtaposed.
The circle does not comfortably conform:
a monk-like shepherd stares off into space;
the long-faced, earthly dad and virgin mom
are beside themselves with more grief than grace.

Everything is set. Someone has been told
to cut the cloth, have angels angle in
to move the man made God up in the world.
All will fall in, the rabbit lope along,
the cock crow, the curled dog be at a loss
to fall asleep, there, at the foot of the cross.

Aidan Rooney

Circuit

Like that pink flamingo not a mile back
dropping its tucked-up leg only to leap
with a great flap to dinner in Bouzigues,

I must have been half asleep or still light
in the head—lunch *Chez Philippe* in Marseillan,
then some Picpoul-paired oysters in Pinet—

when the front wheel went out from under me
in a patch of stone dust. I stayed clipped in,
clattering beneath the bike out front of

Languedoc Agrégats. The helmet kept
my right ear a half-inch off the tarmac
that hummed its racetrack song of passing cars.

A truck stopped to exit, rattled its clutch,
depositing a line of damp pea-stones
smelling of the ash of a fire long out.

I lay there till certain all was right,
the little blood coagulated, my sweat
gone cool, the dark and a hunger coming on.

Lynx
(or poem beginning with half a line by Matthew Sweeney)

i.m. Matthew Sweeney (1952–2018)

Scrape the cat off the road and continue on down
95, the hell out of Millinocket, Maine,
into the snow's hypnosis. Have your partner part
the winter fur on her thick neck, sedate the cat,
compose, for comfort, the great, lovely snow paws
and black rings of her short tail. Get a move on. Pause
once for a blast of drive-thru coffee, then beeline
it to Tufts. Call ahead. Say the job is feline.

Visit through spring. Comb the gray rime from her mane,
massage the buff underside. Once the screws have taken,
bear gifts of bird and fish, cutlets of venison,
endangered snowshoe hares. Rehab on a treadmill.
Come March, monitor for estrus. Bring in a male
to see if, behind the mirror, the cat can move on.

Aidan Rooney

Post-Op

I've pressed the call bell thrice
but no night nurse has come,
rivery mackerel ladder up
my delirium.

The arrows in the armrest
of the jacked-up gurney
fold my legs and lift my chest
up for the journey

peripatetically through the ward's
undead in the dead of night,
ill-lit forms through half-closed doors
slightly pitched upright:

the mangled and the comatose
high-cushioned on narcotics;
the chronic drunks, the over-dosed,
inveterate neurotics.

In blue johnny and sticky socks,
a 4-wheel-drive chrome staff
hung with bags that, in and out,
drip on my behalf

Go There

deliverance from the half-life shape
Osiris ended in,
his insides cut to pieces,
his body parts grown thin,

I parkour the corridors
to be seen to be seen.
In mirror elevator doors
I come across as green.

And then from out the river
under an overhanging tree
a hand pulls on the kite snagged
on every reverie.

Is the pain supernatural?
Can a shade beyond the pale
sweep back the curtain drawn
around my crook and flail?

Aidan Rooney

The Mottoes

You were not necessarily better off
out altogether of the uniform
you were too cool to order from Heatons—

steel, stay-press, very Bryan Ferry trousers,
and an army surplus, cable-knit v-neck
with a velcroed *fortis et fidelis* patch,

and the black and amber-striped skinny tie,
you eejit, you left hanging on a peg
inside the big old, blooming rhododendron,

her her socks up all the way to her knees,
a maroon pinafore, and a jumper
with its *ut sint unum, Dieu le veult* crest,

were you to act the oynie after school
along the path around Saint Peter's Lake,
intent on what the mottoes really meant,

and one of the sisters—Joseph, Trea, Liam—
or a father—McDaid, the Bull McCague,
Red Hand Hanlon himself—to be like-minded,

Go There

on a stroll once about the lake, stopping
the odd time here and there as if to do
a station of the cross or a novena,

or some such observance, then carry on.

Aidan Rooney

The Seventies

Mental strawberries at six and seven.
Turnips. One of the patients after me
with a cleaver. Cider with Rosie heaven.
Eight, nine, jam damsons for Blind Rafferty.
Bringings in. Hay bales, onions to hang, cows.
Minding them up to their bollocks fucking
the same cows. Forever wheeling barrows.
Around ten, trading fags, mag porn. Ducking
into the army tents after the bomb.
Eleven, picking stones. Cement. The camp
permanent. Loving Massey Fergusons.
Twelve, thirteen, 4-Seasons packer. Big Tom.
The Horslips. Headbanging. The odd town tramp.
Fourteen. Freak. Bowie. The petrol stations.

Quiz

Not (a) the neighbours crouching dogs   but (a) clouds
   (b) the gatehouse spinster's hissing cats   (b) planes
   (c) the flock of simili-eponymous budgies (c) butterflies
   (d) the eating-disordered hammy-hamsters (d) stars

I've taken to naming after my (a) loves,
              (b) failures,
              (c) suspicions,
              (d) secrets,
                          always on the lookout

for three together, (a) slouching
             (b) drifting
             (c) shooting
             (d) hitch-hiking
                                   past,
like Magi on the move, calling out for names. Today, some
   usual suspects:

(a) sex : food : wine
(b) the wife : foie gras poêlé : Montbazillac
(c) Mathilde B. : jambon de Bayonne : Pécharmant
(d) Laure de Noves : olives niçoises : Châteauneuf-du-Pape

        dangerously (a) superimposing
                  (b) apart
                  (c) abutting
                  (d) random

    but deliciously shape-shifty as ever, the day not yet
    strapped on, not

a lick of (a) Ishigura
         (b) Celan,
         (c) Chomsky
         (d) Vendler

       yet read, pre   (a) -stretch,
                       (b) -coffee (all sighs and burbles in
                               the kitchen)
                       (c) -run around the block,
                       (d) -meditatively,

   in mid-stoop for the folded (a) GQ
                               (b) Northern Standard
                               (c) LRB
                               (d) Equipe
                                              tossed

   at the driveway's foot and mouth, in too-big slippers

              and a quick wrap of a (a) sari,
                                    (b) tutu,
                                    (c) kerchief,
                                    (d) greatcoat,
                                          given way

Go There

for a rent of sky caught (a) upsidedown
                         (b) rightsideup
                         (c) roundabout
                         (d) arseways
                                              backlighting

my petite pendant (a) relay stick   of (a) religion,
                     (b) bird-in-nest   (b) love,
                     (c) poster-child   (c) war,
                     (d) rubberducky   (d) death,

                                                     such things.

Aidan Rooney

Posts

1. On Religion

Has made his mind up you must change your life.[1]
Is back in Thebes to halt the Bacchic dance.[2]
Urges OMG, take the gentle path.[3]
Holds there is no sin but ignorance.[4]
Joys that death doth touch the resurrection.[5]
Has done his twice twentieth pilgrimage.[6]
Finds fire a depressing destination.[7]
Forgets distance. Comes to the water's edge.[8]
Forgives the Lord Thy great big joke on me.[9]
Is downloading *Shake off the Dust ... Arise.*[10]
Seeks friends to feel solitude more keenly.[11]
Gives thanks to God for dappled things for skies.[12]
Likes Gretchen's post. Asks does not He sustain Himself?[13]
Wonders who can be more wonderful than myself?[14]

---

1. Rainer Maria Rilke (1875–1926), "Archaic Torso of Apollo"
2. Euripides (c. 480-406 BCE) from *The Bacchae,* Pentheus condemns Dionysus
3. George Herbert (1593–1633)
4. Christopher Marlowe (1564–1593)
5. John Donne (1572–1631), "Hymn to God, My God", in *My Sickness*
6. Farid ud-Din Attar (c.1120–1220), "The Conference of the Birds"
7. Muhammad (570–632) attributed, the Qur'an
8. Wang Wei (699–759), untitled
9. Robert Frost (1874–1963)
10. Matisyahu (1979–)
11. Paul Valéry (1871–1945)
12. Gerald Manley Hopkins (1844–1889), "Pied Beauty"
13. Johann Wolfgang von Goethe (1749–1832), *Faust*
14. Walt Whitman (1819-1892), "Song of Myself"

2. On Love

Has heard the mermaids singing, each to each.[15]
Is building a heaven in hell's despair.[16]
Thinks a kiss a trick designed to stop speech.[17]
Wants to sing what a beautiful Pussy you are.[18]
Is sipping a cup of Camomile tea.[19]
Would none had ever loved but you and I.[20]
Is going to some lips of sweeter melody.[21]
Will luve thee still till a' the seas gang dry.[22]
Admits no impediments to marriage.[23]
Will persist. Has boundless desire. Infinite ache.[24]
Plans to arrive in a horse-drawn carriage.[25]
They flee from me that sometimes did me seek.[26]
Has a bad dose of stove and freezerburn.[27]
Will love when nothing's looked for in return.[28]

---

15. T. S. Eliot (1888–1965), "The Love Song of J. Alfred Prufrock"
16. William Blake, (1757–1827), "The Clod and the Pebble"
17. Ingrid Bergman (1915–1982)
18. Edward Lear (1812–1888), "The Owl and the Pussy-Cat"
19. Katherine Mansfield (1888–1923), "Camomile Tea"
20. W. B. Yeats (1965–1939), "The Ragged Wood"
21. Oscar Wilde (1854–1900), "Silentium Amoris"
22. Robert Burns (1759–1796), "A Red, Red Rose"
23. William Shakespeare (1564–1616), "Sonnet 116"
24. Pablo Neruda (1904–1973), "Cuerpo de Mujer"
25. Lady Kathleen, "Cherished Moments"
26. Thomas Wyatt (1503–1542), "They flee from me that sometime did me seek"
27. Francesco Petrarca (1304–1374), "I Find no Peace"
28. Antoine de Saint-Exupéry (1900–1944), *Le Petit Prince*

3. On War

Exhorts: Fie! Shame! How long will ye slumber?[29]
Would not talk with such high zest. The old lie.[30]
Notes: never in one day died such a number.[31]
Roars, at break o' day, let us do or die![32]
Too loves jeans and jazz and Treasure Island.[33]
Can't find his own name in letters like smoke.[34]
Does a great cover of this land is my land.[35]
Is washing armor in Chiao-chi Lake.[36]
Sees the sky in the crater where you died.[37]
Knows what strengthened me, for you was lethal.[38]
Walks up and down in her gown. Boned and stayed.[39]
Let the Hero crush the serpent with his heel.[40]
Loves the smell of Napalm in the morning.[41]
Car bomb. 40 minutes. Coded warning.[42]

---

29. Callinus (mid-7th century BC), "Exhortation to Battle"
30. Wilfred Owen (1893–1918), "*Dulce et Decorum Est*"
31. Aeschylus (524–455 BC), "The Battle of Salamis"
32. Robert Burns (1759–1796), "Bannockburn"
33. Saadi Youssef (1934–), "America, America"
34. Yusef Komunyakaa (1947–), "Facing It"
35. Woody Guthrie (1912–1967), "This Land is Your Land"
36. Li Po (701–762), "Nefarious War"
37. Lam Thi My Da (1949–), "A Piece of Sky Without Bombs"
38. Czeslaw Milosz (1911–2004), "Dedication"
39. Amy Lowell (1874–1925), "Patterns"
40. Julia Ward Howe (1819–1910), "The Battle Hymn of the Republic"
41. Kilgore in *Apocalypse Now*, dir. Francis Ford Coppola, 1979
42. IRA operative, Harrods bombing, London, Dec. 17, 1983

4. On Death

Is thankful that he kindly stopped for me.[43]
Is scared more of the inadequate life.[44]
Wants no sad songs, no shady cypress tree.[45]
Appreciates that phone calls taper off.[46]
Considers it, like life, a beautiful law.[47]
Keeps on wanting. Death is satisfaction.[48]
Will never find the life you're looking for.[49]
Finds the report an exaggeration.[50]
Wonders will it be the same in heaven.[51]
Has gone over to the majority.[52]
Doesn't want to be there when it happens.[53]
Would hate the photos below the balcony.[54]
Hears the curfew toll the knell of parting day.[55]
Holds up his lamp to light you on your way.[56]

---

43. Emily Dickinson (1830–1886), "Because I could not stop for Death"
44. Bertolt Brecht (1898–1956), "The Jewish Wife"
45. Christina Rossetti (1830–1894), "When I am Dead, My Dearest"
46. Johnny Carson (1925–2005)
47. Henry David Thoreau (1817–1862), letter to Emerson, 11 March 1842
48. George Bernard Shaw (1856–1950)
49. from Gilgamesh, circa 2500 BCE
50. Mark Twain (1835–1910), *New York Journal,* June 2, 1897
51. Eric Clapton (1945–), "Tears in Heaven", 1991
52. Gaius Petronius Arbiter (AD 27–66), *The Satyricon*
53. Woody Allen (1935–), *Without Feathers*
54. Brigitte Bardot (1934–)
55. Thomas Gray (1716–1771), "Elegy Written in a Country Churchyard"
56. Rabindranath Tagore (1861–1941), "Peace my heart"

Aidan Rooney

Francis Bacon and the Hen

Men are alike in this:
whosoever gets
a good idea leaps,

as Bacon did, or
so the story goes,
out of the coach

to have a common hen
slain and gutted, raring
to stuff a ball of snow

in the hen's cavity, ice
as good a cure
as salt, and truth

an insufficient end.
He knows exactly
what he's about,

a hand in the bird,
what way Highgate is,
the price advancement

Go There

pays, and for three
listless, snowbound days
he drifts in and out,

feeling the nip of death.

Aidan Rooney

In a Country Churchyard

i.m. Seamus Heaney (1939–2013)

We want him to go out on a high note,
said the gravedigger's eldest son, himself
a gravedigger. He stood back from the edge,
his right foot on the left lug of a spade.
White orchids dressed the rug of manmade grass
rolled out over planks laid across the space.

His father sat fornenst the opened plot,
on a stone wall the sun going down lit up.
It shone on the flowers and warmed the father,
his good cap doffed, his head inclined in rest.
He'd dug for everyone in the graveyard,
Mad Dog even, and the Hunger Strikers.

We haven't told him yet, the son disclosed,
but will when all the fuss is over.
His father's hair, as the poet's used to, glowed
in a sudden, sideways burst of sunshine.
Magnesium burning. And would not let up
no matter the light. Or the light dying.

After tea, the son drove in the digger,
its link-box raised, then tipped, to fill the hole
with shingle scooped from the shore of Lough Neagh.
It fell like the wall of a waterfall.
He watched his father through its thinning veil
get up to get the shovel and the rake.

The Bones

Each trap contains, I hope, more than the bricks
that give it ballast, and the box cargo
of water hoisted from the depths. The cage
materializes, ghost-like, like a kite
reeled in through fog, and drains in an instant
to spider crabs whose legs I have to break,

and three keepers bucking in the parlour.
They have made good inroads on the pogies
reduced to little more than fin and bones
in the bait bag, unhooked and dunked and swished
at arm's length in the water, releasing
its foul, milky contents through the lattice.

The rinsed skull and backbone sink and appear
brought back to life as black, translucent fish
that swim down to the gloom. I like the crash
the trap makes, tossed back on the ocean,
the mesh bag replenished, hooked and rehung
in the kitchen, the lid bungied back down.

Nothing then but buoys that dip and crest
to the clang of a nearby bell-beacon,
riding the same light chop. I would go for a swim,
let the boat float, a rinse and a cool down,
were it not for the cobalt-turning sky
darkening the ocean's epidermis,

Aidan Rooney

and darkening the one-way, funnel door
into the trap's commodious chamber,
dinner ready. I would go for a spin
round Nix's Mate, were it not for Captain Fly,
the freebooter, whose corpse, chained in a gibbet,
was let hang until the bones rattled in the wind.

Sléibhín

for Derry O'Sullivan

Sléibhín (little mountain) is the name given to the black-headed gull. As noun or adjective, sometimes anglicised as *sleeveen*—*sléibhín* also refers to one of untrustworthy character. The *sléibhín* population in Ireland swells in summer when the birds, otherwise white-headed, don dark hoods.

I dare not leave the edibles outside
behind my tiny home on Blackrock Road
overlooking Crowley's Lounge and Bar backfield
five farmed-out blackface sheep have sheared
for fear that some *sléibhín* black-headed gull
might off with one in its beet-red bill
and end up rummaging in the bin
out back of Box of Frogs in Bridewell Lane
for one of those decadent Maltesers
(biscuit-caramel-chocolate squares)
let melt this afternoon in high sun that showed
the not-black at all but brown-plumaged hood
the sleeveen white-headed gull puts on
on the flight over from France or Britain
to skim these milky skies and vie for scraps
in the clipped back gardens and alley skips.

Acknowledgements

Alabama Literary Review; Carte Blanche (Quebec Writers Federation); *College Green; Crannóg; Cream City Review; DoubleTake; Harvard Review; Horizon Review; Irish Pages; Irish Times; The Lonely Crowd; Mediterranean Poetry; One; Metre; Mudlark; Poetry Ireland Review; Poetry Porch; Poetry Review; Post Road; Prairie Schooner; r.kv.r.y Quarterly; Revival; Salamander; Tanbou/Tambour; The Recorder; The Rialto; The Shop; spoKe; The Stare's Nest; The Stinging Fly; The Sunday Tribune; Verbal Magazine.*

"Angel" received the Daniel Varoujan Award from the New England Poetry Club in 2012.

"Notice" was published in a festschrift for the 30th anniversary of The Gallery Press.

I am indebted to Marc Vincenz for seeing the light in this collection. Thanks must go out too to Bill Tinley, a faithful first reader over more than three decades, and Daniel Tobin for much of the same and for writing a sanctifying introduction. Gratitude, finally, for other friends, colleagues and family who too stand by. I am especially indebted to Hammond Journeaux for her visual translations of the four fables after Jean de la Fontaine. Hammond lives in West Cork, and her work has been exhibited in Ireland, England and New Zealand. She has illustrated the work of several authors, most notably Aine Connor, John Heath-Stubbs and Derek Mahon.

About the Author

AIDAN ROONEY was born in 1965 in Monaghan, Ireland, and educated at Saint Patrick's College, Maynooth, National University of Ireland. A resident of the U.S. since 1987, he lives in Hingham, Massachusetts, and teaches at Thayer Academy. He was awarded the Hennessy Literary Award for New Irish Poet in 1997, and his collections—*Day Release* (2000) and *Tightrope* (2007)—are published by The Gallery Press in Ireland. In 2013, he was awarded the Daniel Varoujan Award from the New England Poetry Club. Widely published in Europe and North America, his work has appeared in various anthologies, *Staying Alive* (Bloodaxe) and *180 More* (Random House) among these. *Go There* is Aidan Rooney's first U.S. book publication.

www.ingramcontent.com/pod-product-compliance
Lightning Source LLC
Chambersburg PA
CBHW020335170426
43200CB00006B/394